FIRST
FLIGHT

Marcus Andersson

This book belongs to:

_____

Today is the first time I will fly through the sky.

Soon, my family and I will board an airplane that will take us on an adventure.

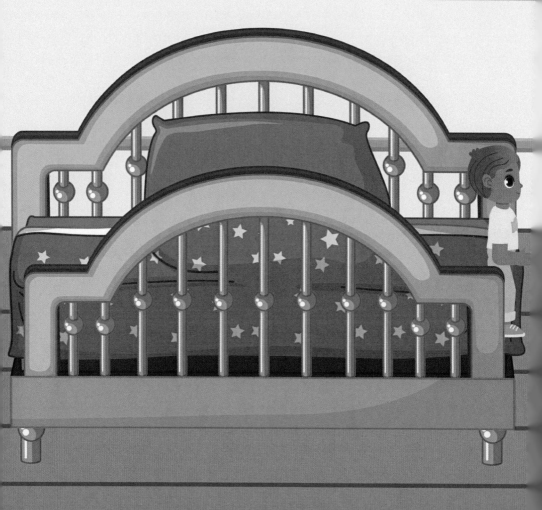

But before we leave, I must pack. I pull out my luggage that has wheels on it.

This will make it easier to move through the airport.

I pack everything I am going to wear. Shirts, pants, and even clean underwear.

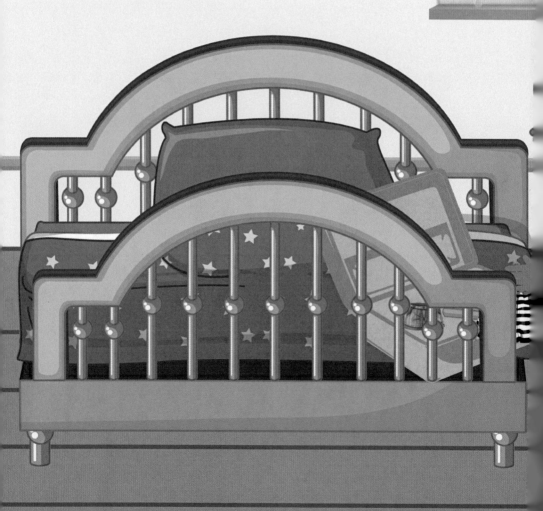

I'll ask mom and dad what kind of weather we can expect, so I can be extra prepared.

I can't forget toothpaste and a toothbrush. And it couldn't hurt to bring some dental floss too.

Next, I need to pack up my carry-on. This is the bag that I will take on the plane with me.

I choose a backpack because it is easy to hold on my shoulders.

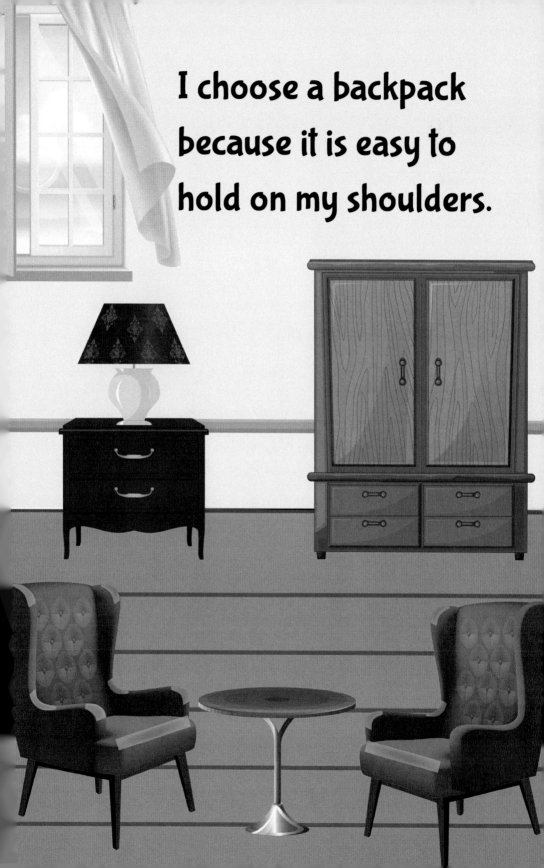

I'm sure to load up my bag with activities to keep me entertained while on the plane.

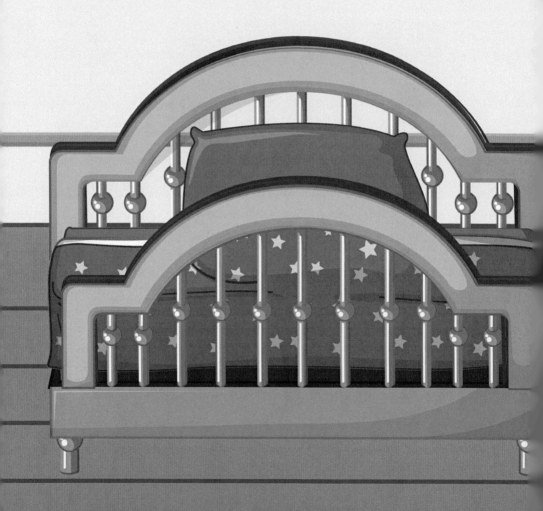

I grab my favorite books, my handheld video games, and a few extra snacks.

Now that I am all packed up, I am ready to leave for our airport adventure.

I set everything by the door. Good thing I made sure to get a good night's rest before we left!

Next, we are ready to load up the car. I help mom and dad put everything into the trunk and then we are ready for take-off.

We arrive at the airport two and half hours before our flight is supposed to leave.

We do this so that we have enough time to check our bags move through airport security. There may be long lines.

We first print our tickets and check our bags.

Airport staff will weigh our bags and then tag them.

Luckily each of our bags was under 50 lbs.

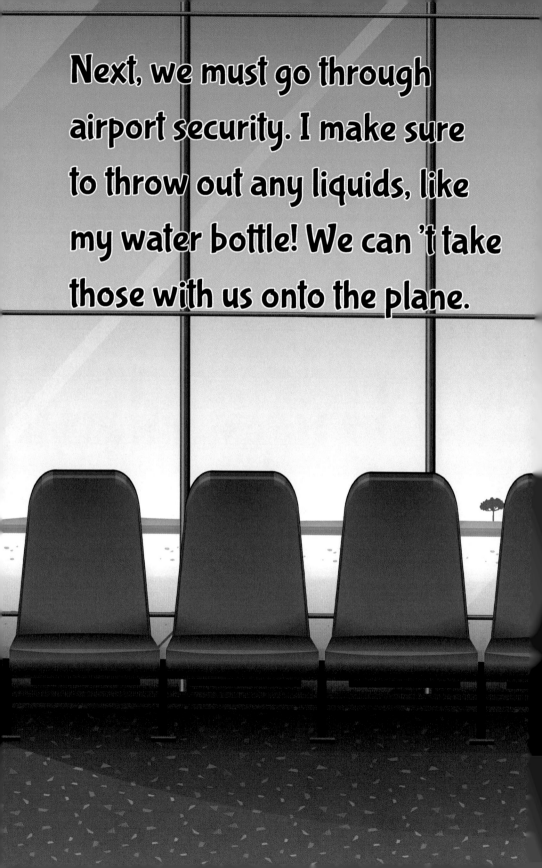

Next, we must go through airport security. I make sure to throw out any liquids, like my water bottle! We can't take those with us onto the plane.

We stand in line for just a bit and mom and dad explain to me that TSA is the airport security. And TSA stands for Transportation Security Administration.

Finally, we made it to
the front of the line.

I must put my carry—on backpack in a bin along with my shoes and belt. They go through a scanner so TSA security agents can look inside. Then I go through a scanner myself.

Once I make it through, we are officially in the airport terminal.

We start to walk towards our plane number listed on our tickets.

Since we arrived early, my family and I have just enough time to grab a quick breakfast.

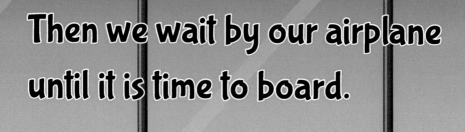

Then we wait by our airplane
until it is time to board.

We will know when it's time to board because our number will be announced on the intercom.

I get excited when it is finally our turn! Our tickets get scanned and we are ready to step onto the plane.

When we get onto the plane,
we find our seats that are listed
by number on our tickets.

We are ready for takeoff! Now that we gone through the airport, we are ready to arrive at our next adventure.

But I remember to listen to the emergency tips that the flight attendant explains, and I feel safe.

For a moment I get a little nervous.

Once I find my seat, I buckle myself in and I secure my bag under the seat in front of me.

The End

Made in United States
Orlando, FL
21 March 2023

31285595R00029